Grandma Used to Say

By Jennifer Bisram-Gould

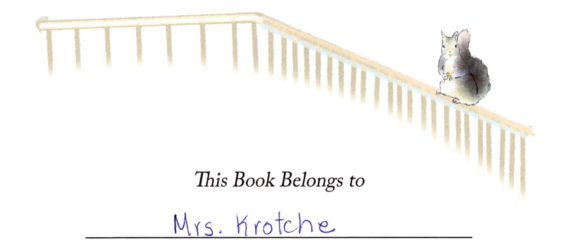

This Book Belongs to

__Mrs. Krotche_____

copyright 2022

*Dedicated to my son,
Alexander Duranjaya Gould -*

*In loving memory of my grandmother,
Bhagmania Ragnanan, who Alexander never got the
chance to meet.*

Grandma used to say,
wash your hands, to keep the germs away.

Grandma used to say,
make the bed, before you play.

Grandma used to say,
be compassionate, especially on
Christmas Day.

Grandma used to say,
pray.

Grandma used to say, family is important, never betray.

Grandma used to say,
share your toys, crayons and clay.

Grandma used to say, "YAY!" when her kids and grandkids visited on her birthday.

Grandma used to say,
look for the sun, even when
the sky is gray.

Grandma used to say,
help others, with food,
a dollar or place to stay.

Grandma used to say,
be kind to animals,
even if they are stray.

Grandma used to say,
do good in school, when you
get a job, you'll get good pay.

Grandma used to say, exercise and your health will be okay.

Grandma used to say, don't raise
your voice at others in any way.

Grandma used to say, tell the truth,
every day.

Grandma used to say, "I Love You," every day.

The End

About the Author

Jennifer Bisram is an award winning
television reporter.

She was once a teacher and published
her first children's book
First Day of School: Do You Want to be My Friend?
in 2014.

She lives in NYC with her husband, Andrew
and son, Alexander.

CPSIA information can be obtained
at www.ICGtesting.com
Printed in the USA
BVHW021331060422
633551BV00002B/30